ISBN 1 85854 776 8
© Brimax Books Ltd 1998. All rights reserved.
Published by Brimax Books Ltd, Newmarket,
England, CB8 7AU, 1998.
Printed in Spain.

Nature's Magic

by Lucy Kincaid
Illustrated by Lynne Willey

B r i m a x · N e w m a r k e t · E n g l a n d

Introduction

We don't have to go to the jungle to be explorers. Jake and Sarah are explorers every time they go out to play.

It is very easy not to notice what is happening right under your own nose in your very own garden, or in your best playing place.

Jake and Sarah are always asking questions when they see and meet something new. By doing this they learn about wildlife and the environment they live in. They find out how to care for the environment properly.

If children have an interest in the natural world, they will develop an awareness of their environment and the need to protect it - just like Jake and Sarah did.

The Storm

Jake and Sarah often took Billy for long walks in the woods. He liked sniffing at trees and searching in the bushes.

If he saw a rabbit, he didn't know whether to chase it or run away from it. He liked to hide and pretend he was lost, but he always came when the children called him.

One night when the children were in bed, the wind began to blow. It blew and blew and blew. It howled around the house and rattled the windows.

Outside, in the darkness, the trees creaked and groaned. Billy didn't like it at all. He crawled under Jake's bed. Sarah hid her head under the covers.

The next morning when they took Billy for his walk, the children couldn't believe their eyes. All around them were broken branches and fallen trees.

Uncle John and his friends were piling up the broken branches and clearing the paths.

"What has happened?" asked Jake.

"The wind has blown the trees down," said Uncle John.

"You'll never move this one," said Jake, pointing to a very big tree trunk which had fallen down.

"We're not going to," said Uncle John. "We are going to leave it where it is."

"But it is right in the way," said Sarah. "No one will be able to get past it."

"We'll pick up its branches and make a path round it," said Uncle John.

And that's exactly what they did.

Woody

Uncle John told the children to watch what happened to the tree trunk.

Every day when they took Billy for his walk, they stopped to look at it. Uncle John had said it wouldn't be long until ants and beetles and other creepy-crawlies started to move in. He was right.

"I can see a beetle," said Sarah one day. "Look, there he goes."

Billy was sniffing under the log. He was sure he could smell a rabbit.

"Someone has been digging a hole," said Sarah. "But I can't see anyone inside it."

Jake jumped up on to the log and ran along it with his arms outstretched.

"I'm the King of the castle," he laughed.

Jake's foot slipped and he fell off the log.

"Are you hurt?" said a strange voice.

"Er...er...no," said Jake.

"Who are you talking to?" asked Sarah.

"Him," said Jake, pointing at a tiny man with a beard and a pointed hat, who was sitting on a twig swinging his legs.

"Who are you?" asked Sarah.

"I'm Woody," said the little man.

"What are you doing here?" asked Jake.

"I'm looking after the log," said Woody. As if to prove his point he jumped down from his twig and spoke to the leader of a column of ants.

"Hey! Hey!" he said. "Not that way! That's already full. The beetles moved in yesterday. Follow me. Attention. Quick march."

The children watched in amazement as Woody marched off in front of the ants. He led them down the side of the log to a dark, earthy space underneath it.

"I think you'll find that much more suitable," said Woody.

"Thank you," said each one of the ants as it disappeared into the hole.

"That was kind of you," said Sarah as Woody climbed back onto his twig.

"It's my job," said Woody. "Someone has to make sure everything goes smoothly with so many new residents moving in. Can't have any quarrelling can we?"

The children could see now why he sat on the twig. He could see exactly what was going on from there.

Every day more and more insects and creepy-crawlies moved into the nooks and crannies of the log.

Woody was kept very busy keeping everything in order. He seemed to have eyes everywhere. He saw everything.

One day Sarah saw a baby bird sitting on the path, quite close to the log. It was looking very lost and very lonely.

"Poor little thing," said Sarah, and she bent to pick it up.

"Stop! Don't touch it!" shouted Woody. They had never seen him look so stern.

"I'll be gentle. I won't hurt it," said Sarah.

"Leave it where it is," said Woody. "It doesn't need your help. It is waiting for its mother."

"But its mother might not come," said Sarah. "Then what will happen?"

"Its mother will come," said Woody. "And we will watch over it to make sure nothing happens to it before she gets here. Sit here with me, and be quiet."

Sarah and Jake sat on either side of Woody. They watched and waited.

Soon Billy came down the path sniffing. He saw the baby bird. The baby fluttered its wings, but it didn't know which way to fly.

"No, Billy!" said Jake sharply, catching hold of Billy's collar and pulling him away. "You mustn't do that. You will frighten it."

"Well done," said Woody, approvingly.

Woody shooed away some beetles who had come to look. They hadn't meant any harm.

"It's just a baby," said Woody. "It's waiting for its mother."

"I wish she would hurry up," said Sarah. "It must be getting hungry."

Just as Sarah was beginning to think the baby bird's mother would never come, she finally arrived.

"There, what did I tell you," said Woody.

"Cheep...cheep," said the baby bird, fluttering its wings and opening its mouth.

The mother bird dropped a caterpillar into the baby's beak. Then gently she coaxed it into the tree where she had her nest. It took a little while because the baby had just learned to fly and could only do a little bit at a time.

"You were right," said Sarah.

"Of course I was," said Woody. "How else would the baby have gone back to the right nest?"

"Mother always tells us to stand and wait for her if we ever get lost," said Jake.

"It's the same for birds as it is for children," said Woody.

Goodbye

By the end of the summer the big log looked as if it had been lying on the ground for years. Woodland grasses had grown all over it. There were families of ants, beetles, and centipedes living in the log's nooks and crannies. There were rabbits and mice living in burrows underneath it. It was as busy as a small town.

One day as Sarah and Jake were on their way to visit the log, they saw Woody on one of the winding paths that led deep into the woods.

"Hello, Woody," said Sarah. "Where are you going? Can we come too?"

Jake was looking at Woody's backpack and his walking boots.

"Are you going away?" he asked.

"Yes," said Woody. "It is time for me to get on my way. My work on the log is done. Everyone is living happily together. There is no more quarrelling. It's time I found another log to sort out."

"But why?" asked Sarah sadly.

"Because that's what I do," said Woody.

"Will we ever see you again?" asked Jake.

"Who can tell?" said Woody. "But thank you for all your help. Now you can look after the log for me." And with a cheery wave he disappeared round a bend in the path.

"I suppose if he has work to do, then he has to go," said Jake.

"I suppose so," sighed Sarah. They had learned a lot from him and were both going to miss him.

Fishing

Sarah and Jake were lying on the bank beside the stream. They were trying to catch a fish.

The fish was twisting and turning and darting this way and that. Each time Jake thought he had caught it, it escaped.

"Got it!" he shouted at last. He held up the jar.

"What kind of fish is that?" asked Sarah.

It was the right size for a minnow and it had a proper fish tail. But it also had arms and long, streaming hair.

"It's a mermaid!" gasped Sarah.

The children's dog, Billy, was sniffing the jar with his wet nose.

"Go away!" shouted a tiny voice.

Jake was so surprised he dropped the jar.

"What are you staring at?" the mermaid asked angrily.

"I've never seen a mermaid before," said Sarah.

"How did you get here?" asked Jake.

"I escaped," sighed the mermaid.

"Where from?" asked Jake.

"From a storybook of course," said the mermaid.

"Shouldn't you be in water?" asked Sarah anxiously.

"And whose fault is it that I'm not?" snapped the mermaid. "You took me out. You put me back."

"Don't put her in the stream," said Jake quickly. "She'll swim away and we won't see her again."

The mermaid didn't like being inside the jar.

"Let me out. Let me out now!"

"Will you stay in the stream if we do?" asked Jake.

"I might," said the mermaid with a toss of her head.

"Will you come if we call you?" asked Sarah.

"I might," said the mermaid with a flick of her tail.

"Will you promise to come back tomorrow if we let you go?" asked Jake.

"I might," said the mermaid.

Jake was holding the jar a little too close to the water. There was a sudden flash of silver and the mermaid was gone.

"What a dive!" gasped Jake.

Would they ever see the mermaid again? They hoped so, but they would have to wait until tomorrow to find out.

To the Rescue

The next morning the children were up so early that there was still dew on the grass. They raced to the stream.

"Coo eee," called Sarah softly. "Are you there?"

There was no answer. Perhaps it had all been a dream after all.

"Woof," said Billy softly. He had heard something. Now Sarah and Jake could hear it as well.

A cross, little voice was telling someone to keep still.

"Where are you?" called Jake.

"Stop asking silly questions and do something," was the mermaid's reply.

Billy jumped in the water and paddled towards a patch of water weeds.

Jake waded in after him. The mermaid was struggling with a fish in the weeds.

It was holding onto her tail. She was shouting at it to keep still.

"Let go of her," shouted Jake.

"Don't be silly," said the mermaid. "I told it to hold on. It is tangled in the weeds. I am trying to pull it free. Don't just stand there - do something."

Jake pushed about in the weeds with a stick.

"How did the fish get so tangled in the weeds?" he asked.

"It thought it could show me - a mermaid - how to swim," scoffed the mermaid. "It swam round and round, faster and faster until it caught its tail in some weeds and couldn't swim at all."

As Jake poked about with the stick, the strands of weeds began to float apart.

At last, with a tired flick of its own tail, and a hard pull from the mermaid, the fish was free. It swam away without a backward glance or a single word of thanks.

"It might at least have said thank you for all the trouble it caused," grumbled the mermaid.

"Maybe it was embarrassed," said Jake.

The mermaid sat on a stone and inspected her tail.

"Is it damaged?" asked Sarah.

"I'll know when I have tested it," said the mermaid. She dived off the stone and was gone.

Sarah and Jake waited for a very long time but she didn't come back.

"I wonder if she has a name?" said Jake.

"I'm going to call her Chloe," said Sarah. "And I'm coming back tomorrow."

Snow

The children saw Chloe almost every day throughout the summer. Then the days began to get shorter and colder until one morning the ground was covered with a thick layer of snow.

Jake knew exactly what Sarah was thinking because he was thinking it too. Was Chloe safe?

They raced to the stream to find out.

It was very quiet and still everywhere.

"Where is she?" sobbed Sarah. "Chloe, where are you?"

"What is this white stuff?" asked a cross, little voice.

As they caught sight of her, a drifting snowflake landed on her head. It looked just like a hat.

"It keeps doing that," she shivered. The snow was melting and trickling down her face. "It's cold and I don't like it."

The snow was melting all around her. A drip fell onto her head and exploded in a shower of droplets.

"That keeps happening too," she grumbled. "It's not safe anywhere. I'm starting to feel very dizzy."

"We'll dig a hole in the bank and make you a cave to sit in," said Jake.

Holes! Billy knew about holes!

Soon there was snow and mud flying everywhere.

"Stop!" shouted Chloe. Mud was running down her face and sticking in her hair.

Billy took no notice of her. He was an expert. He would only stop digging when the hole was how he wanted it.

When he thought the hole was big enough he stood back and wagged his tail.

"Well done, Billy," said Jake.

Chloe sat in the cave and looked out at them all.

"The snowflakes can't get in, and even if the snow drips all day it won't drip on you in there," said Jake.

Chloe watched the snowflakes falling and watched the drips dripping outside. She felt snug and safe.

"It will do," she said. "Thank you, Billy."

Ice and Icicles

The next day it was even colder.
There was a thick layer of ice
on the stream.

"Oh, poor Chloe," said Sarah
when they reached the cave.

The dripping snow had turned
to icicles, and the icicles were
blocking the door of the cave.

Jake wanted to laugh, but
he didn't dare. He broke off the
icicles instead.

"You can come out now," said Jake. But Chloe didn't come. She wasn't in the cave!

"I can see her," shouted Sarah. "She's trapped under the ice. She can't find her way out."

Jake quickly made a hole in the ice. But instead of waiting to be scooped out, Chloe swam right past them and back under the ice.

"Poor Chloe," said Sarah. "She's frightened. She doesn't know what she's doing."

Jake made another hole.

"Slow down," gasped Sarah as Chloe sped straight across the space in the ice and back underneath it again.

"She was laughing," said Jake. "She's not frightened at all. She's playing games with us."

There was a giggle behind them. Chloe popped her head above the ice.

"Can't catch me," she called and was gone again.

Billy tried his best but he became tired before she did.

"I knew you couldn't catch me," said Chloe popping up right beside him.

Quick as a flash, Billy licked her up with his tongue.

Billy sat with his mouth open, not knowing what to do next.

"Put me down," shouted Chloe, hitting him on the nose.

Jake came to the rescue. It was hard to tell who was more relieved - Chloe, Billy or the children. What a calamity it would have been if Billy had swallowed her!

Chloe thanked the children for rescuing her and then waved goodbye.